The Stunt Double in Winter

poetry by Robyn Art

THE STUNT DOUBLE IN WINTER

ROBYN ART

A DUSIE BOOK * 2007

Many thanks to the editors of the following publications, journals and anthologies where many of the poems herein, some in earlier versions and incarnations, first appeared: 88, *Alice Blue, Big City Lit, canwehaveourballback?, Cocunut, Conduit, Convergence, Good Foot, Hangman, NoTellMotel, Rhino, Redactoins, Red China, Segue, Shampoo, Skidrow Penthouse, Slant, SLOPE, Tarpaulin Sky, The Burnside Review, The Hat, The Saint Elizabeth Street Review, The Shore, Terminus, Unpleasant Event Schedule,* and *Wicked Alice.*

Selections of the poem, *The Stunt Double in Winter* appeared in the mixed media exhibits *Spontaneous Art* and *Peace works* Times Square Lobby Gallery, NYC.

The Love of the Body was featured in *Crossing Borders*, an improvizational concert performed by the Newcastle University, Australia.

The Stunt Double in Winter also appeared as a limited-edition text/visual chapbook from *Dancing Girl Press* in 2007.

The author would like to acknowledge the lifting of lines in way of the title and first/last lines in the poem, *This Thorn Bush, My Thorn Bush*, from William Shakesspeare's *A Midsummer Night's Dream, Act 5.*

First Printing, Robyn Art, 2007

Non-commercial reproduction of this work is permitted and encouraged. Reproduction for profit is prohibited except by permission of the author.

ISBN : 978-0-6151-8262-9
Cover Art: MAKE ART NOT LOVE, by Marianne Morris, reproduced here with her permission.

Cover Design and layout by the editor in Adobe Garamond and 1942 Report.
Dusie books are published by Dusie Press,

: Dusie Press : Zürich, Switzerland :
: editor@dusie.org : http://www.dusie.org :

HOMO SUM, ERGO NULL' ALIENA EST.

(I am human, therefore nothing is foreign to me.)

I, with crashing consequity, waited, wanting
to have experienced many, many things.
                              Lyn Hejinian

for my parents

IMPRESSIONS FROM
THE UNREAL CITY   13

THE STUNT
DOUBLE IN
WINTER   33

MIDNIGHT IN
THE SURGICAL
THEATER
61

LIVES of the
PHANTOM LIMB
77

HANDFASTING
IN SPRING
93

What I love most is the idea of the meadow. Next the meadow itself, the proffered ground and its rows of itinerant weeds. Then the idea of "I," then saying "I have" in a blizzard. Then the meadow again, the wind-driven leaves and the measured hills in the distance. I have to stay. I have to watch until the sun blots the taxed horizon beyond this coliseum wall. I have to wait for a "this." My idea is to remain standing at all times, even though they mean to flog me behind those ionic shafts. I mean to rouse the wounded. I mean to ogle the flayed ruins and their semblances of woe. Then the night's sidereal awning, the stripped, mimetic clouds. It's this humming that wakes us, this irretrievable light. The idea is to have. I too was mucousal once, housed within a pliant vessel accustomed to my demands, then shunted through a passage incommodious beyond all reason. If you must, unfurl my sutures by the rain-besotted rose. I'll never be forgiven for regaining the shape of my skull. It's this humming that wakes us, this irretrievable light. What I love most is the idea of the meadow.

Impressions from the Unreal City

THE CENTRIFUGAL AGE

Sometimes it starts with a single word and sometimes that word is *volvox*. Caution, surface hot. Do not force or fracture. As we have learned from its slipshod dabbling and heavings of wood and lead the body never tires of any blunt or weighted object. Do you dream much. Have visions. On a Lotto ticket once, I swore I saw the face of the Lord. At this juncture, feel free to move about the cabin, e.g., ambulate, masticate, gestate, fornicate. Like other animals, we tend to lick and carry our own. Some places it's always night. Bear up, bear down. Not darkness, just the thorough absence of light. Somewhere along the way, I've picked up some useful things; mainly, you don't describe the ambience by something it is not. Also, strike out the inessential, e.g., Press-On nails, Schnapps, the effluvial what-have-you's. I mean essential in a relative sense. It's true I enjoy escapism in pretty much any form. Particularly if it involves the acquisition of rain gear. Have you ever lost control of your mental faculties. That is, gone blotto. You can tell me, I'm a trained professional. By now, most of my kind have vanished into the hills. Apply pressure with circular strokes, as if tracing the alphabet on a grain of rice. Do you smoke. Take this man. Me, I believe we shed our casements like any other deciduous species. In pursuit of the spiritual life I avoid loud patterns, call waiting, most dishes produced with lard. My bout with TDM led to an ongoing altercation wherein the soul cashes checks on the body's tapped account. Please return seats to upright position. Favorite position: Warbler-Hovering-in-Maytime-Cherry-Blossom. Like many of you, I've dreamed of the simple life where I can pursue the art of canning. If not canning, any pastime involving a trowel. Warning, hour is near. Breathe in, bear down. At this time note my omission of certain instructional data, e.g., by what means thread the filament through the body's lattice of holes. So far, so long, O lifetime's attenuated whatnot. So when did you learn to whistle. Bury your old dumb loves. Transcribe the windfallen scriptures and proclaim them your wildest dreams.

JEDI MIND TRICKS

Cusp: final round

Permeate: tell me how that makes you feel

Harbinger: the water unsafe

Apple: as in, of my eye

Luteal: and on the seventh day she bled

Certainty: any smooth, uncluttered surface

Gradient: the hotdog stand is thataway

Mailing address: between her magnificent thighs

Transformation: competitive rates

Carapace: pace of a car

Hemorrhage: the eager wages of night

Fulgurate: gimme gimme gimme

Surcharge: we regret to add

Vestibule: resinous, dewy

D-cup: feeling of unusual closeness

Handshake: don't be alarmed

Lacustrine: all has been transformed

Idea for a story: sun actually rises

Waver: her beautiful, lachrymose mouth

Situation: wanted

Missionary: touch me there

Certainty: wicks away moisture

Virtual Lockdown: the Resurrection has been postponed

Stroke: some assembly required

Nocturne: no skin no breath

Follicular: been feelin' them blues

Yours: most likely to---

Clairvoyant: embossed with dew

Worst Refrain: you can't win em' all

Barter: patchwork smocks

Latency: story of my life

Certainty: foals with the heads of angels

Angels: foals with the heads of certainty

Proximity: hot   hotter   hottest

Somnambulism: decent form of exercise

Idea for a story: all have been forewarned

One is: one is only

THE INSOMNIAC IN WINTER IMAGINES A VISIT FROM OUTER SPACE

Now is when the motor cuts
in the glade of nebulous calm,
the swath of oaks drawn close

against the on-ramp's harkening shudder.
Beyond, the glow of the Quicky-Mart

peddles its stock
of No-Doz and swabs,
cavalcade of gauze to staunch
the body's myriad leaks.

Far off, on another street,

his children, tubbed and fed
tumble deeply
toward the night,
his wife, redolent,

tousled,

dreams of palm trees
and life before Kegels.

Now, against the fibrillant tide of Trazadone,
Reiki, bourbon, acupuncture,
valerian, Sega, Shiatsu

and Gilligan's Island;
now would come their questions
below epistolary stars:
Where is your leader?
Can you describe the vehicle in question?
What can you tell us of this fruit?
Can you delineate the markings of loved ones?
Do you expect it will be long?
By what manner will we know them in the torn
and wind-lashed fields?

TRACE

In the beginning they had no name for it
so they called the animal "Night."
How they loved to band in the distance
to witness the great head roar.
By degrees it appeared to soften
and a new sound piped from its jaws.
In the meadows. And in their dreams.
Muted. A sort of keening.
Being less afraid they began to come to the animal alone.
How lonely I am they would whisper to the shadow
of its massive flank, or *Lately I've had these dreams.*
Sometimes they would croon to it in the syllables of their kind.
By degrees they decided "Night" was all wrong
and they renamed the animal "Longing."
How it appeared to fathom their sole desire
to be of a single flesh. They told the animal secrets.
Ergo, it grew omniscient, having heard tell of their withered plots
like so many grapes on the vine.
In time the animal revealed to them
philanthropies of its own. It appeared to know a thing or two
about the cultivation of peas. It would wipe a woman's febrile brow
as the head of her progeny crowned.
They were amazed at the animal's lack of disgust
for the trappings of their kind, e.g., blood, offal,
excrement, amniotic leakage; in short,
all corporeal substance of origin. Thus they drew their counsel
and renamed the animal "Kindness."
In time the animal took on certain features
of their race, e.g., this one's penchant for whittling;
that one's munificent breasts. Indeed it began
to walk among them in its own inviolate likeness
to the syllables it had garnered in the early days by fire.
So adept at this the animal was
that eventually they grew frightened.
Of the footstrike. And the roar. And the ponderous,
thudding heart. Hence they drew the animal out

and turned it loose in the fields.
Their eyes trained on the progress of its wretched,
vanishing bulk, past the deadfalls and the tree-line
as the alluvial wind sharpened.
Thus they returned to their spackled lives to raise and bury their own.
By degrees they grew accustomed to the absence of the roar.
To what no one could have told them.
 That the animal would not cease.
That they would quicken at its waking as if from flame
issued forth from a single flesh.
In the meadows. And in their dreams.
Muted. A sort of keening.

NOTE FOUND IN THE POCKET OF MY OLD HYDRO-VAC SUIT

For awhile, I couldn't do much.
No one was eating mussels,
then mussels were O.K.
Suddenly, it was pork you had to watch out for
and one day, I woke up in my Teleport chamber
to hear on the radio that the vibes were all off,
something to do with Saturn rising so what I had
to do in here was re-arrange the chairs.
"Eat more mangoes" my friend advised
but there were very few mangoes to be had.
I had these feelings of inferiority
but turns out they weren't the right kind.
And all this time,
the sun heaves its massive loneliness
across the clouds as if we won't all
betray each other in the end,
the expired husks of stars blinking out
in the vitreous dark.
I hung out at the dunes a lot.
I had this skin you could see right through.
So much Tri-Galactic Void
through so much mnemonic ash--
You posted somewhere in Voltron Eight
and me so in love I could die.

THE TWO

When they were able by degrees to move without pain,
    the detritus settled, the celibate whiteness gone, the two of them

all a-tremble, that is, scared shitless; when it became apparent that it wasn't yet
    the end, no, mayhaps a tic in the backlogged agenda

of the Authorities, content as the two were to let bygones be
    bygones they reckoned they were not without their captors in light

of all that had come to pass: their truant desire like nothing before it,
    the diastolic wherewithal of his blood, the sole objective being pleasure;

true, they had not, as of yet, begot a lovechild,
    but erstwhile violated the conditions of their parole, the

monumental pissing contest of which they wanted no part,
    their greatest crime being love, the indecorous

rustlings beneath the fronds; how could they know to what scope
    it would all be laid waste: banished without end to the lesser kingdom,

its office parks and methadone clinics; its lube jobs, Snack-Shacks
    and centers of mass entertainment, their kind heretofore doomed

to the insatiable fits of longing for which
    they would risk all matter of denouncement, punishable by Law,

that is, subject to strip-searches, therapeutic dosing, and the like;
    yes, disperse as they would to the hinterlands they would never

surmount their longings, the indexical offenses for which
    they would suffer dearly; of all of this the two would never

be absolved, their visitation rights denied, their sole objective being pleasure;
    O what a crazy trip it was, the acres of green before them,

just after the first light unfolded, just before the singing began

NO LONGER A BLONDE

It's all mostly gadgets now
and pre-packaged rice

the ten-year-old in platform mules recalls,
when I was a kid

still the body like an adder's tongue in its single
chthonic desire

Botticelli's women: necks arched like swans,
thighs locked like Alcatraz

did you manage to fit in the wing chairs and how
did you feel about leaving

this technique may cause discomfort, yes,
but it hurts real good

boys we knew have cut their hair
and launched careers in Finance

do you know much about those petals
falling from your mouth

and we shall be fruitful and cruel to the end,
sad but true

Botticelli's blue man: extreme
sexual frustration

no one's eating shellfish
lamé is again in fashion

how'd you like this juniper bush
rammed down your throat

definition of loneliness:

approximate distance from you

the right hand doesn't know
what the left hand's doing

turning into a tree of sorts-
she's no longer a blonde

"Other" is my best bet
from the list of occupations

definition of regret:
all the dumb stuff I've said

some women turn into knockouts,
some turn into shrubbery

used to be you'd spend hours just
unbuttoning my jeans

spring's competing desires: sudden yen for vacuuming;
urge to swallow a rose

the long drive southward
our love nearly gone

the idea is to rotate lengthwise
add saliva as needed

all has been forgiven, nay,
all has been transformed

the dark worm prods its nubbled head
between the leaves

IMPRESSIONS FROM THE UNREAL CITY

There were meant to be so many things—guaranteed parking—resurrections like clockwork—extended hours of operation—there were to be any number of libidinous displays—Monies allotted by the State—there were to be various diversions—various schemes—there were to be debts forgiven—the Authorities behooved to act graciously—meaningful gestures out-of-wedlock—complimentary oven mitts—there were to be conferred honorary degrees—opportunities for engorgement—aid for those befelled, broken-hearted, or shit out of luck—incentives for the exodus—windfalls blown hither and yon—they could continue in their way—keep on the Help—suffer periodically from bloat—above all—they would never have to be lonely again—there was that much—the nearly asphyxiating joy—yet—sometimes in the stillness—they would think the durndest things—tearing the perforated edges—strolling the decimated parkways—what the wind was saying—how their mommas lied

BECAUSE LIGHT ITSELF IS A NUTRIENT

Because light itself is a nutrient she's out
each day at noon,
trekking from the overpass
to the poke of stringy elms.
The bloom cannot be salvaged,

nor the roar of progress stopped.
How many times
she has pulled to the shoulder,
transmission shot to hell.
Been the nom de plume,

the one in blue,

scribe at the shotgun wedding.
Had she the words she'd tell a daughter,
Go in fear of the nine-to-five.
Be familiar with love and cruelty
and apt to confuse the two,

and always,

take pains to maintain the body's
delicate balance of water.
Because distance cannot be measured
between this world and the next
from some blighted holler the dead

call out, blotto with childbed fever.
She will measure the nearing hour
by the tulips' genuflection toward night

and the traffic slowed on the off-ramp,
potholes glutted with rain.

Now is when she'd tell her girl, Fall far,
stumble freely.

Fashion a staunch and unswerving hunger
for the integrated life.
And should the spate of disbeliveers
sound their ballyhoos of doubt
stay low,
strike early,
take the long way home.

PSALM

Because they were starting to go funny
From living so long alone,
Being as they were bodies of impenetrable light,
Perchance a trick of the eye,
Perchance a spate of gaseous matter,
Because it was mighty cold up there on the Mount,
Being as they were luminous, winged,
Omniscient in that particular way of the Chosen,
Because they would not have us await the acquittal
All by our lonesome, charged as we were
With multiple counts of cluelessness,
Caught out in the fulminant glow of the Ubiqui-Cam,
Because they would forgive us our calamitous elections,
Redemptions-by-mail, In-boxes
And cheap thrills, because they would forgive us all
In our singular fulcrum of need,
Because all along the evacuation route they have never
Left our collective side,
Have followed us to the strip mines, skin flicks,
Places unrenowned for their verdancy,
Have climbed with ua onto the table
And endured the insertion of unheated metal,
Have cramped, have seen us through both our night sweats
And our dopaminergic afterglows,
Because they have pitied our fruitless bouts
In the Bliss-Simulation Chamber,
Because it always has been thus,
Their whispered analogs above our heads,
The all-abiding darkness,
The neonate taking seed

THE FEMALE'S INCARNATION AS A RING OF SALT

does not acquiesce to the face peel,
nor shy away from fleeing the house
bedecked in any old thing. Does not object
to the notion of pork rinds,
of getting shitfaced on Holy ground,
cannot confess to any battered dreams
of revamping the County hall.
Could never accessorize, quick-step,
or sauté for love or money,
nor would it be wont to appear of its will
in anything resembling a truss.
It confesses to dreams of snow squalls,
truck pulls, hightailing it to Vegas,
things it was fixing to grow,
the endless reel of fanzines
detailing life beyond the slag heaps......
Rumored to be touched,
it never had a head for figures,
thrice it has called for a retrial
and thrice it has been denied,
getting on in years,
tending its row of hosta,
shaved within an inch of its life

NATURE IS AN ANGRY MACHINE

Who feels no pain upon insertion: Whose light-stippled
Hours ricochet past the wet and clover-strewn fields:
Who affixes with names the lucent shimmerings glimpsed
Beneath the blade: Whose immeasurable shadow lengthens:
Who confiscates the loam: Whose Tilt-A-Whirl the earth
Hurls through the vortices of stars: Who retreats to the myriad
Backcountries of its own entropic design: Whose indigenous petals
scatter all the way to your hotel: Who delights in yanking the plug
on that ruinous: Shell the moon: Who witnessed the fight go out of
the Good Fight Due to lack of adequate funding: Who glistens with
indiscretion: Who abideth not the word: Who will laud the undulant
sky: And soldier on among the missing :

BLOOD-LETTING

not the body
not the seed
not the deleriant fog
not the hillside
not the dictaphonic birds
not the well-nigh impossible road to the sea
not the lovestruck
not the bemired
not the kinfolk
not the deleriant birds
neither the body
nor the labile squandering of its seed
neither the sea
nor the fog's impossible body
not the mammiform hillside
not the pro re nata flight to the sea
not the labile
not the seed bereft of its kinfolk
not the flight
not the well-nigh impossible fog
neither the hillside
nor the pro re nata squandering
neither the kinfolk
nor the labile birds
not the road
not the deleriant body
not the impossible
not the mammiform seed
not the dictaphone
not the fog
not the lovestruck body
not the dictaphonic road to the sea

WISH YOU WERE HERE

It is not now as it hath been of yore.
Still the bracken lashed with dew and the moon's
redemptive shadow,
still the heart's tepid cockles thrum
with manufactured glee.
Still today was generally a good one,
as we told them at the desk—no internal bleeding,
no entrails squashed on the glass and if we shifted
our gaze that sewage pipe was just
a clot of ferns, that lack of pulse a catnap
in our ectoplasmic scheming.
To take my mind off things I tried tripping through the copse
but mine vernal, wreathed bower is now
the smoking section of Hal's.
I kinda like staring at the perforated sky
where the city drops away,
unanswerably alone, always darkness
falling outside or darkness falling inside,
the wind's pneumonic wheezing
or the body's numinous cage.
Maybe if I'd just held you beneath those plastic elves,
something convulsive shrieking in the space above our ears,
my skin a nest of wires, sodden, murderously alive
in the enormity of night
and its lexicon of betrayals.
There were all these zapped hydrangeas.
I wouldn't sleep for days. The overpass racket was nothing
next to the wingbeats in my skull.
When one has been long in city pent.
When one has pent such longing.
And how long it has been such,
O my city of longing, my pent one.

THE STUNT DOUBLE IN WINTER

As there are no walls that can hold it it is apt to feel quite lost. Ibiden, it has made as such a lifework of its flaws. There are still things it would state for the record: name and place of employ; its fraudulent knowledge of Rolfing; off-the-clock diversions and its prowess at five-card stud. Many would love to see its tongue cut out, an end to its smarmy asides; it has dozens of uses for patchwork and as many words for grief. If caught, it would shatter. If held, effloresce. Mark its words, if it ever were to lose the appeal it would air-kiss its way down the gangplank. Let it never be said it hasn't a tale to carry with it to the grave.

Although the body never marries
it enjoys its share of rubdowns
observes itself from a distance
through its scaffold of desires
the body feels most at home
in the banked repose of hillsides
it can view itself too clearly
in the grasslands and the flats
once the body believed itself
above the realm of scouring
now it scours in earnest against
the threat of going soft
the body's greatest comfort
is its dogged state of pulsing
its singular concern
is in keeping itself intact
rarely the body tries its hand
at astral communication
it relinquished quite some time ago
the search for its long-lost twin
still it trolls the self-help aisle
for tips on co-dependence
(although little abates the body's
pervasive fear of going soft)
over time the body learned
to micturate on schedule
yet still it remains clueless
as to how to lay down tile
for the most part the body doesn't buy
the notion of an afterlife
little it trusts of anything
it can't store on the shelf
still the body has its questions
as it emerges from the shower door--
Are we allowed the illusion of wholeness and what
are the principle uses of myrrh

(ON HOW THE BODY GREW INTO ITS DORMANCY)

It is not love the body asks for
but evidence of its capture,
the hierarchy of sloughing and ripening,
the sleep which is the body's recompense,

for days now it has been without urgency,
nary a twinge of the quickenings
which had defined its hours thus far,

even so, the body in abeyance

is not easily hoodwinked, not by design,
not by the flight of its fugitive cravings,
it has become adept at disguising its latency,

just so, it postures by the wet-bar, adjusting its straps,

angling a hip so as to appear wanton,
even so the body in its torpor,

not fecund, not fallow,

in lieu of its hankerings it has its Lotto
and its travel plans in the offing,
it will now and then bestir itself

to troll the supermarket aisles, untempted
by the profusion of luncheon meats indeed
the body keeps its own hours,
has no use for the exigent timepiece,

will go forth, just so,

with all intention of being fruitful
but on the bifurcation of its species
the body is of two minds,
will touch itself covertly to be sure

it is still extant, de facto,
still the body in arrears,
betrothed to its indenture,
whatever shall it do for a ring

Why does it all take so long: why the safe room why the backstock of sensual aids why must it be haunted thus by the oneiric quackery of its dreams why the sod why the rapture it will pay back in spades why the sun on the ruins why the handle when it has no hands why the avoidance of radon and transhydrogenation why the comorbidity of its wants and its needs   Oh it could tell you stories   it is haunted by visions of water of being called upon to operate the electrelocephelograph machine   something about the rain something about the house lashed clear to the sea oh why has it labored thus why the mood music and tranqs why its grunt work in the capitol why its stroke-mags Nag champa speed-dial and Evacu-Pak why the nefarious specter of saddlebags something about the meadows something about the wild and luminary grass something about desire or anhedonic lack thereof it has been awhile since it has moistened or sallied forth of its own volition despite the inebriant sky despite advances in Teleportation something about wisteria something about the light Oh Lawdy yes it will have its heyday yet

THE STUNT DOUBLE IN WINTER

Because it has been without solace for some time now
it has honed its multivalent wants to a scarce
and thrifty few: A solid chair;
a finer margin to its days.
It can remember taking a lover of sorts,
long long ago,
though it feels itself to be singularly alone and this
it concurs with some relish.
Oh, it used to know so many things—
the principal exports of Guam,
how best to collect the dew.
Here it putters around the domicile
with its view of the chemical plant,
recalling its glory days in the capital,
its blacked-out, dopey fumblings
in rooms beyond repair, that time
when it was held beneath
the ruinous mantle of dusk.
Because it was once one of us,
it has a working knowledge of physics,
knows to lean into the fall
and cover its head against the blast,
erstwhile it knows what it is,
to you all it bids a fond Adieu—
a bush in which birds are singing,
a window streaked in ash.

THE STUNT DOUBLE IN ITS WANDERJAHR

If it had a nickel
for every time it skipped its bail
it could subsidize the feckless

from here to kingdom come.
Plums by the roadside, skin like milk,
the aphasic fall-outs and Be-Ins

of its misbegotten youth—
rooms it has forsaken
but for thumbprints on the wall.

Quo ad hoc some will venture
it's a shadow of its former self;
freeway-wizened snowdrops

in a vast, unquiet ground.
Along the way it collects brochures
and tepid renderings of the view;

it still enjoys the occasional fete
though at long last it has lain down its arms.
Through some sleight of hand

it has managed thus far
to dodge the mandated tithe
as well as the out-of-wedlock yearnings

that are the tools of its demise.
 Oh what season bereft of flower
it has had to endure

beyond hope or reason
in the backwaters of its past.
Wonder of wonders it has gotten this far……

Once the body was limber

and could scramble through the bracken

now it takes its chances

with the lurching subway doors

sometimes in the turnstile

as it clasps the bag of Cheetohs

it has the vision of cupping berries

in its scarred and eager palms

the body misses drumlins

and the perks of having a tail

it hoards its fading wildness

in its window sill of herbs

over time the body learned

to circumvent its longings

it has become adept at filing

(though it refuses to multitask)

the body is unflagging

in its sole pursuit of freedom

it credits the tenuous woodlands

and the invention of Caller ID

the body does not wish to stand

affixed beneath the headpiece

what it wants is drumlins

and the perks of having a tail

the body has grown weary

of the need to Make It Happen

nor does it harbor the patience

to Take A Holistic Approach

although the body enjoys an omelet

it cannot abide the embryo

too saddened by its birthright

(read: its sadly vanquished tail)

if pressed the body is ready

with the necessary data

it can name the city's highlights

with the necessary glee

the river here is brilliant

(though it wouldn't drink the water)

the architecture stunning

(though it wouldn't breathe the air)

And so it transpired that the body grew unruly, gradually and by degrees refusing the mithradite, usurping the counter staff, going braless, staging protests and benefit luncheons in the name of surmounting its captors, i.e., those who would the body genuflect, remain seated, exit by Stairwell A and above all sidestep the trappings of its own corporeal likeness, this after all has always been the body's greatest weakness and hence its greatest joy, it cannot restrain itself from restroom mirrors, convenience store windows, or from fashioning its likeness from the teratogenic dyes, so enamoured the body is of its own intractable logic it has long refused to pick up its mail, appear in a court of law, show up at the appointed time, it has long since waived its right to an attorney and all conditions of its unconditional surrender to which the body has its own rebuttal, that being it will not violate the terms of its own inviolate likeness which is the body's greatest weakness and hence its greatest joy, will refuse all offerings of parking tokens, iron lungs, tract housing, reduced rates, roadside plums and all gifts proffered for its unconditional surrender, the body has a mind to falsify its records, it will drag out its trowel and transplant the zinnias, will multiply, nullify, i.e., will not go quietly

Because it cannot escape its meanness   the body discovered weeping

it got the hang of walking   through its quest to reach the grapes

it zoned out all day on the bookcase and that the body called   thinking

this it found the hardest and vowed to limit the practice thereof

the body relinquished its turgor   and hence discovered sleeping

it learned to permeate one of its kind   and knew it was onto something

gradually the body learned   to harness its betrayals

and navigate the freeways of its own   factitious needs

still the body is often vexed   by the weight of its decrees

it resents its corporeal trappings   elimination on demand

the body engulfed the bowl of rice   and that the body called eating

this the body relished   and vowed to increase the practice thereof

the body has picked up certain things   such as how to tie a slipknot

or fashion its own likeness   from the teratogenic dyes

although the body will never forgive itself for its lasting failure to aviate

it is proud of the thing it has learned to do   by flailing its limbs in the pond

the body found out the hard way the pitfalls of running with scissors

hence the body was reprimanded   and considers itself warned

sometimes the body will catch itself   in the act of recrudescence

thus the body discovered breathing and its most   enduring trick

(THE SOUND OF THE BODY)

Body thought sound for tree

Body thought push-up bra   and vestiges of moonlight

Body thought hillsides   besotted and swept with dew

(Body tried sound for want   and came up with hover

and likeness   and is)

Body tried for subtlety   but lost it by full dilation

Body tried for vociferous longings   cloaked in truck stop coffee

Body grabs the set of keys   and floors it through the night

Body covets New England spring   and its livelihood of verdancy

(Body tried sound for want   but got lost in the consummate pears)

Body doesn't just happen   it knows from its mapwork of veins

and the lists it keeps for birthdays and mulch   on the battered freezer door

Body thought sound for ocean   and its seat of benthic desire

(Body tried sound for want   and came up with idea for theme song)

Body considers bequeathing its limbs   to the ductile swathes of wind

Body fails to speak in tongues   due to fits of giggling

(Body tried sound for want   as it ambled along the freeway

Body   trying to amble   wanted   to sound in the way of the free

the sound of longing tried the Body   its ambling of want

but free   the way   the body ambles

along the freeway   wanting)

(ON WHY THE BODY REFUSES TO MARRY)

There are still wonders it longs to behold: Devil's Tower at sunset; the world's largest wheel of cheese.

There is no love lost between the Body and the bellicose nature of its kin.

Because its bloodline cannot be traced, to all those who have swindled the Body or done it irreparable wrongs, it means to make good on its word and the word will not be pretty.

Because of Rocky Road, county fairs, the last vestiges of its youth in the floodplains.

Because at intervals it must be kept away from sharpened objects, knives chief among them.

Having been eighty-sixed or otherwise banned from its customary haunts, its locus in quo, place of skull-- the Body now smoked from its lair.

Because the Body never carries what it cannot break with its own two hands.

Plain as the nose on its face, plain as the day at the morn.

The Body being no fool, its approval ratings up, is savvy to the role of aesthetic in its continued domain of the homeland.

It prefers to be tousled in light, knee-deep in standing water.

To the fallible logic of the Five-Year-Plan, Tri-Lateral Plot, wheat grass colonic or stowed flotation device, the Body offers up its bottomless glut of counterfeit charms.

Because like anything, its will can be bought and sold.

Because it is short on time, long on demands, and hungry for the silence that is the Body's paramour.

Because it has traveled places where it could not see the sky, could not partake of the stream, where even the roll of toilet paper was under lock and key, the ever-present lockdown in which it has made its home, the Body has its demons though it is loathe to say as much.

Because the Body is a one-horse town, and a bit of the wunderkind at that.

And because the Body has long considered itself a gifted raconteur, it has left no stone unturned in the peripatetic byways of its girlhood, the rote, eternal crib-sheets of its being thus far, the marriages, abdications, ingestion of contraband substances to which it has oft borne witness, the dry-rot infestations of its big dumb dreams and the vision in which its love is coming toward it through the rye-- so little the body has left to the public imagination, why had it believed itself free, and with the fight left in it yet, Ah, how it wonders, whatever could it have been thinking

The body carries its longings beneath   the architecture of sky

it spreads the blanket, masticates the sack of finger sandwiches

the body has its hobbies, among them, forming hives

it can be found ordering a Mai-Tai   dispersing leaflets on toxic waste

admiring its fields of striated flesh   in string bikinis and chaps

mostly the body tries to ignore   its wheel of subtle wreckage

it keeps itself busy   with the perpetual sorting of mail

it likes to think of Inner Peace   it has several entries for "Yard Work"

sometimes the body dreams   of hovering over the freeway

sometimes it wakes   to the fleeting scent of zinnias

always it walks with the muted threat   of being punched with holes

the horde of weevils burrow   in the marrow and the soil

still the body takes its pleasure   in the rows of planted beans

soaring rents conspire to drive   the body from its houses

I want to see the lake again   it muses to itself

but the body isn't leaving,   not for love or money

although sometimes it takes umbrage at its   inability to fly

On good days the body's skin

is blotted with the scent of lilies

on others it contemplates waxing

or moving out-of-state

sometimes the body stares into space

or whistles the theme from M*A*S*H*

it longs to get down on its haunches

with the earthworms and the offal

the body enjoys trying out

new salads from the cookbook

sometimes it whispers endearments

to the enumerated dark

saddened by the vanishing meadows

it likes running by the marsh at twilight

the body is often weary

of its continual Need-To-Know-Basis

the body enjoys descending

from the labial cellar doors

to the shelves of roots and plums

where the body stores its loneliness

at times the body questions its need

of unremitting light

I have toiled in the blood of the Lamb, it says,

Now where's my free dessert

Aside from the disparate rages that are the stock and trade of love and the perpetual crash-and-burn of its Big Picture plans it will admit to few regrets from its salad days of yore, hours of plunder and ruin replete with attendant phantoms for hire, unctuous appeal of the roadhouse and escapist joys of the strip-mall, in praesenti what the body takes for its prodigal shit from Shinola and what it would make a run for with only the clothes on its back—tomatoes put up in the fall; long drives to books-on-tape; times it has wondered in secret, how much further to the sea.

First the lake

        then the dream of the lake

first the corrugated night

        then the night's endless revisions

first the blood

        then the gradual ebbing thereof

first the wood

        then the wood fingered with bracken

first the word

        then the word's tremulous shudder

at once the dread of wind-sprints

        and the love of the excellent pain

first the presence of salt

        then the slow emergence of water

first the close of the shutter

        then the terrifying likeness

first the feel of his thumb

        then the wonderful nuance of pressure

just as the womb is opened

        so the womb sharpens its longings

just as she loosens her sash

        so his sash of desire unfurls

first the voice

        then the gradual ebbing thereof

you are the lake   you are the dream of the lake

THE LAMENT OF THE BODY

The body disguised its feathers

since then it has had no visions

the body discovered petting

since then it has had no rest

since the body eluded death

it's been obsessed with the plight of the ficus

since the body took up Keno

its concentration has been shot

often the body resents its cage

and must be coaxed through the doorway

often the body moans aloud

from its bed of pilfered sleep

now that the body is getting on

it limits its intake of nougat

the body loathes being required to speak

in the requisite manicured verbs

once the body vacationed

since then it has dreamed of water

once the body tried stealing

since then it has had no hands

PRIMIGRAVIDA

Ever doubtful of its ontogeny, having so often missed the sign for the on-ramp, been fustigated for its golf swing, vitriolic comments, marked down in all matters of comportment as well as for the pot with vulcanized oatmeal, tub with soap-scum, etc., the Expectant One comes to rest, albeit with the full onus of its fecundity, awash in the teratogenic half-light of the X-ray station, an open magazine on its soon-to-be-vanquished lap, although the Distended One, as of late caparisoned in hip-huggers, g-strings, and all matter of belly-tees wonders how it got itself into this imbroglio, escrow of its womb, at least it can no longer be slandered a cocktease although it has of late neglected to shave, its bikini line has positively gone to naught, it reminds the Aqueous One too much of the inevitable exit wound, compresses, sitz baths, yes, thinking of this the Fecund One is prone to tremors, still it rolls along on its jangle of nerves through the day's infernal to-do's, it has no wish to become ineffectual, grow porcine, although it sometimes must be coddled, feeding on vittles heretofore deemed revolting, it can as of late be found sprawled fully-clothed beneath the covers, in situ, saddled with the massive weight of its faticity, no longer the monthly spasms, jettison of its linings, the Tumescent One is wary of, yes, downright fears, the disrobing upon entry, rupture of membrane, feigned insouciance, the flimflammery of the pre-Op, it wishes to call a halt to the proceedings, abscond to the Snack Bar, address the housing crunch, curtail the unmentionable burden, ravenousness, withholding of Downtime, it doubts not the body's potential for expulsion, it is positively full of holes, still, the Primigravidic One wonders how it got into this imbroglio, it had its pick of inseminators once, was known on occasion to binge-drink, preen, downright cavort, moisten in public, overcook the rice, admit its ignorance of the Hedge Fund—no, it cannot recall its life in the tar-pits—yes, even then the mark was upon it

The body reclines in a wing chair in a dilated shaft of light

it ponders the question of dinner   while combing its lacustrine hair

at times the body cannot abide   the tenor of its loneliness

it has wearied of carousing   and its depilatory needs

it longs to begin the day   with the fall toward another body

it does not wish to consider   the requisite falling-from

still it reclines in its wing chair   combing its lacustrine hair

it ponders the question of dinner   and the dilated shaft of light

the body is transfixed by the process   whereby one body begets another

it knows to lie very still beneath   the thrashing of its kind

alas   the body harbors doubts as to its own lactiferous yearnings

will the Market retain its firmness   likewise   its nalliparous thighs

this the body ponders   from its dilated shaft of light

as it combs through the question of dinner along with its lacustrine hair

when the body is forced from its wing chair at the light's ineluctable rupture

it pauses in the breezeway   to examine its split-ends

Will the weather hold the weekend   it ponders aloud to no one

through the evening's pulsed dilation   and a shaft of lacustrine hair

THE STUNT DOUBLE IN EXILE ON THE EVE OF THE BODY LAID WASTE

For once the Other stalled on its own intractable wheel,
at liberty to unwind, that is, suspend all plans to attack,
not returning phone calls, not tweezing,
not perusing the Notions aisle and all manner
of accoutrements, something deep within it
settling like a house on its studs, relieved albeit briefly
of its perpetual fear of sinking, the continual drawing-down
within the hour's soporific drone,
the quickening, the cramps all through the night,
evidence abounds at will that yes
the body was here, (see Hair in Drain,
see Tinge of Blood on Sheet) the body qua the body
in the ponderous bulb of its birthright,
demarcations of water and blood,
the aegis that is bone,
the body and its Other having endured together
so much, all supernumerary come-downs,
curettage, managerial shit-for-brains, inexorable
spanning of state lines, destination nowhere fast,
the resolute falling toward or is it
the resolute falling from......

And so it happened that one day the body no longer wished to remain agile, that is, it retained its admiration for the state of being agile yet no longer vaunted agility as its sole pride and joy, raison d'être, part and parcel of its life thus far as documented by its collection of magnets, punctured socks, shoebox of fulsome receipts, pamphlets, hashish, languno, backs of folding chairs, Ramen, Pyrex, torn flesh, scampi, fugal hum of its cells, (i.e., epidermal, ovarian) strip malls, teething rings, someone named Yarrow, all of which have provided the body with a context of sorts, useful as reference points within the long story of its reification, a story the body never wearies of telling, in particular to members of authority, e.g., airport personnel, when asked to provide documentation, e.g., actual blood coursing through the vein, at which the body is apt to take offense but from which the body also takes a certain degree of comfort, it is being asked for the long story of its reification, a story the body never wearies of telling and will continue the telling thereof so long as it remains upright, ambulant, adept at whist and the fashioning of its likeness from the teratogenic dyes, for this the body has endured chest pains, penury, the chronic rash of its birthright, all in the name of its perpetual reification for the body holds little stock in the afterlife although it can, if prodded, recall the hedged outlines of a past life as a pair of tongs, it does not care to contemplate its future life as a mime, there are things for which the body has little patience, furthermore, things the body loathes, e.g., organ meats, chapped lips, positioning its feet in the stirrups, twin-sets, hotels with no A/C, all these the body has suffered in the name of its reification although it cannot be counted on to meet even the simplest demands, having been demoted on several occasions for its failure to levitate, ovulate, pay the suggested amount, wipe the febrile brow of its kinsman, of course the body cannot be held accountable for the air raids, it has never learned to aviate, plagued as it is by residual cottonmouth, dry heaves, breakthrough bleeding, locchia, has oft been accused of being enuretic, ammhenoreic, part and parcel of its long reification whereupon it has been forced to flagellate, annunciate, and waltz under duress, yet the body has remained steadfast, it has thus far refused to name names save for those pertaining to the long story of its reification, a story the body never wearies of telling, it cannot be blamed for this pleasure, held accountable for the missing, the destruction of the meadows, rising as it did from the sink of effluvial mud to claim the chronic rash of its birthright and begin henceforth the long story of its reification, e.g., all the places the body can be found, e.g., loitering in the stairwell, poultry farming, arguing the finer points of volleyball, traversing the county line, divvying up the landlocked masses, manning the Sno-Cone machine, shuddering deeply beneath one of its kind, part and parcel of its long life among the lesser bipeds although the body is not without its detractors, i.e., those who would the body become weak, chastened, receive its weight in chain letters but for its detractors the body has ragwort and the long story of its reification, a story it never wearies of telling even as the body is slackened, refuted, dispossessed of its frippery, made to verify in its own hand the long list of conditions for its unconditional surrender, even still the body remains upright, ambulant, in possession of a certain je ne sais quoi, skilled at stud and the cultivation of snap peas, part and parcel of the long story of its reification, charges of philanthropy to which it pleaded no contest, point of no return, for which the body does not care to leave a forwarding address

THE DREAM OF THE BODY AT THE LAYING-ON OF HANDS

the pulling	the rising	the falling	the touch
the being	the wording	the touching	the word
the having	the wording	the pulling	the pull
the falling	the having	the doing	the done
her hand	his mouth	her wanting	his want
torque	penetrate	oscillate	filch
the one	the only	the taking	the take
chokehold	pupate	nightshade	cleave
the having	the being	the wording	the word
the pulling	the falling	the rising	the touch
the being	the touching	the wording	the fall
the pull	the pulling	the rising	the rise

(ON WHAT THE BODY WAS THINKING)

(Somethin' 'bout whippoorwills   somethin' 'bout yon auriferous coast

'bout desire flush with lack thereof   'bout certain unassailable rights

somethin' 'bout kickbacks and the rabbit's thorny asylum   somethin' 'bout antigens, Foosball, multilateral banjax,   Day unbeknownst to the Night   and the munificent province of tongues

somethin' 'bout the free-for-all   'bout the ululant ghost of his voice

somethin' 'bout jailbait and the secret life of hoarfrost   'bout walking amongst the felled the negged proposal for armistice the ill-fated go at the hemp trade and snow, waking up to it all blowin' round

somethin' 'bout his fingers   'bout the murdered wetlands

'bout the metaphastic lives of the Chosen and the Doomed

somethin' 'bout a whole lotta nothin'

somethin' 'bout the flogged and wind-beleaguered plains

'bout his face at the all night dive

'bout the loveshack known as Sleep

somethin' 'bout violets breakin' clear through the rock)

Of all it has learned in its own good time—
of those states that would do no harm
that would laud the body and harbor it—
of all it remembers of fire drills
and the badlands of its Inner Child,
it can count on one hand the times it has triumphed

or gotten by on its looks,
those modulated blah-blah-blah's on which
it has hedged its bets. It has seen others falter,
actually die of love.
Nights, it goes forward with its lachrymose ablutions,
the moon a footloose animal

burrowed through with eyes. By and by
it has grown weary but passably wise
in the ways of amour.
Whatever it has gleaned
from its sojourns through the heartland
is not enough to relieve it

of its sole desire to vanish.
The way she held her head,
spot checks at the border,
the carnivorous fanlight of stars—
Some days its mind goes wandering
like something set loose in the fields.

Here is the lamp, here is the chair,
the oft-indentured phrase book
without which it would be quite lost—
Care for a drink,
Don't make me do this,
My my, just look at the time....

MIDNIGHT IN THE SURGICAL THEATER

Tell me again how the story begins,
the light withdrawing,
how the body grows
gradually useless. Here is the paper,
here is the rock,
here is the sun en route
to its smokeless
and luminary burning.
Somewhere it is always
the breath drowning,
the fog rolled in continuous
coils off the sea.
And somewhere it is always
the place from which
the drowned breath emerges,
shuddering,
the way it never does on earth.

EXIT WOUND

And everything that is found there;

    And the magnanimous rustlings of trees;

And the vast and omnivorous silence,

    Mute phone in an empty room;

And the light's residual plunderings;

    And what is the nature of your emergency;

And the past's ensnared carcass,

    And all that is naked and kicking;

And the panic grass and wildflowers

    Around the broken trailer steps;

And the infant's lactiferous tongue;

    And the thunderous What-Have-You's;

And the one saying *I am so lonely;*

    And the gorged subsidiaries of rain;

And the lovers absconding to the hills;

    And the backless, strapless, and low-rised;

And the tremendous and constellated night;

    And the befuddled architecture of clouds;

And everything shot with green;

    And everything—everything shaking

ON THE EVE OF THE SOLAR FLARE

Here in the lesser kingdom the living
greet and pass through,
loving and failing each other in all

the usual ways.
Rooms stand empty, their people afoot
in the blank and snub-nosed dark

for the cause of the greater Good that is
the body sprung from its trap.
The skyline trussed as if within

some grander fiefdom of need,
pages gone unread like beds
no one has slept in.

When the storms came,
there would be nothing
in their wake left standing:

Not the houses,
not the trees, not the hands
they would put their hands to.

SHOTS FROM MY LAST SURVIVING B-FILM

Watch him touching her lightly on the shoulder

as they enter the restaurant, watch the muscles

of his forearm clench as he reaches

across the bar, watch his hands

grip the wet architecture of the glass and imagine

it's the wet architecture of her body, in the shower,

gripping his, imagine someone (him, in fact)

coming toward someone (you, actually) in the endless,

slo-mo tickertape of your triple-X dreams,

imagine a pain like splitting,

the stub of a nail bitten down past the quick,

imagine the slow, dry-heave burn that is

the unventilated orifice of lust, picture a soaked rag

stuffed in the lion that is your mouth, now imagine

it duct-taped shut.

Now imagine eating.

HYPHERPHASIA IN THE DRY TOWN

Outside, the cloud's torn scraps,
snow like curdled milk
raked with a trowel.
Moon a perfect exit wound

in the lightening morning sky.
She pours the coffee into diner mugs
an orthopedic-shoe beige.
Touches his hand. Neither one of them

getting any younger.
Inside, their bodies glide past each other
in the well oiled and noiseless ease
of the married and the dead.

The hogtied wages of love: Hair
on the pillow, flower
through rock, scuffed-up slippers
with the tags still on.

EVENING IN THE FALLOUT ZONE

If the body has a saying, *C'mon
in, the water's fine,* if the spaces
around it could talk they'd sound like *Caution,*

surface hot. This far
from the searchlights,
nothing stays put: shirts run;
hair uncoils form its trappings;
the dead put on their best and stroll
the halls of the body's long house.

If love were a padlock,
it wouldn't hold.

It lets the phone ring, preferring
the gospel of one body
in the other.
It won't smoke, preferring
not to whither.
Meals at all hours; her reddened

lips; the night sky's maculated face
in which the moon will hatch
its luminary plots against the sun.

Skin cools, the dog runs off
in his sleep. Friend, I know water

will flow from its source
though you'll notice I've got
but the one good eye.

SECRET B-SIDES OF THE SONG OF SONGS

Music to rattle your gourd to
Music to maul the Beloved to
Music to maul the beneficent effigies of the Beloved to
Music to quiver astoundingly to
Music to breathe through a rubber gorilla mask to
Music to mangle the apparatus to
Music to stroke the cloistered thighs of strangers to
Music to assemble -the -hand truck- while- fully -engorged to
Music to finger appendages to
Music to stroke the faceless multitudes to
Music to say I-love-you-and-can-I-ram-this-
head cheese-down-your-throat to
Music to smear undulants across the haunches of the Faithful to
Music to sustain moisture-related injuries to
Music to ream the corporeal corridors of your soul to
Music to jostle purposefully to
Music to swaddle the meat of infamy to
Music to heave against flesh-hillocks to,
Then leave through the broken door

THE DOPPELGANGERS OF SLASHER FILMS

Here is the scene where they're pulling
the ransacked bodies from the car,
the sunset a spreading bruise

like the woman's punched-out eye.
Here is the lipstick, here is the dress,
here are the small betrayals going off

like hand grenades, here is the body
bent double over the toilet bowel filled
with blood. Here is the woman

throwing back pints of the Two-fer-Tuesdays swill
as men's eyes slide over her
like overripe meat over hooks,

and here is the scene, at last, of awaiting
the lover on a country road—killing
the scorched out engine, watching

the roach clip skyline, thinking of pulling his hands
to your white-hot throat and what
could be keeping him

NOTES ABOUT HIS HANDS

Could I even tell how it was,
his hip on mine against the wall, my hands
shaking, had I ever touched him that
way in some other life, was his skin
always so hot to the touch, the shirt
I shoved my hands under;

Could I even touch him how he was,
shaking, my hand against the hot wall
of his hip, had I been
his shirt in some other life, was I always
so hot to the touch like something
he would shove against;

Could I tell him to make it even,
my hip shoved against the wall
of his hands, shaking, had I always
been so hot in another life to tell
how it was, to be the skin
under his touch;

Could I even tell his hip from my hand,
shaking, had he ever
touched me in some
other life, was his shirt always a wall
against my hand, could he
shove my under

*

Amorous: hot breath, the bra unfastened, skin like a nest of thorns,
scent of wood smoke, milk, a tussle of decomposing leaves

Savage: did not attend the termination

Redundant: the couch, the beer

Savage: this won't hurt a bit

Amorous: the bodies of women on trains

Redundant: don't ask me again

Savage: hot breath, the bra refastened, skin like a nest of thorns, rain, the shape of water

Remorseful: the flowers, the beer

Remorseful: Yours, Truly &

Redundant: the leaves are back on the trees

*

(What to Do When You Can't Forget His Hands)

Order your steak bloody, your whiskey, straight up.

Purchase sensible things you've needed for some time: ink cartridge, rain gear, vacuum-cleaner bags.

Picture him tasting the congealed frosting of wedding cake samples, talking to the blonde-tipped florist, checking his watch every fifth word.

Remember all the places his hands have (haven't) been and all the places you wish his hands have (haven't) been.

Take long baths.

Make dinner for the man you live with. Manage (a record) not to burn the sauce.

See him everywhere: hotel bars; the laughter of people on trains; the dopey, blanked-out eyes of the Krispy Kreme guy.
Floss.

Take to drinking sherry in the tub while leafing through women's magazines. Learn to mulch, prevent rug burn, undo a zipper with your teeth.

Buy a rubber plant on sale. Manage (a record) to keep it alive for a month.

Recall, in the dark, the warmth of his mouth on your neck, the warmth of his neck on your mouth.

Picture him, again, the only way you know how: standing around the portico, fumbling with the lighter, his shoulders hunched against the wind and beyond him the water, always the water...

*

(Elegy for his Hands)

It was late, I was drunk, you were warm
to my hand, I would say, please
don't leave, touch me there, but
you never

I was late, you were drunk, it was warm
to my hand, I would want, just
to please, you were there, but
I never

I was warm, you were late, it was drunk
to my touch, I was just
late to want, but I would
leave you never

*

MIDNIGHT IN THE SURGICAL THEATER

In the cone of blue light
the opened human glistens,
silvery and rare
like the guts of a tropical fish.

Here is the scalpel,
here is the hand,

here is the body devoured by light.

Beyond the floodlit room
the slow hemorrhage of minutes
into hours, months into years,
blue sky into formless,
unfathomable black.

If only love, like oxygen,
could save us.

If only like ice it could break,

shiver,

leave only the barest trace.

FOUR TREATMENTS

Sky like an unlanced boil. Eyes like broken glass. Beyond the abandoned glove factory, the gray and immeasurable river. A shiver in her voice. Hair like dead leaves. The moon a balled-up fist. Mauled years burned down to the roach.

*

Sky an abandoned gray. Eyes like fields of scabby ice. Beyond the mauled hillside, the smokeless and immeasurable burning. A roach in her voice. Hair like a shiver the dead leave. The moon an unlanced boil. Years a river of balled-up fists.

*

Sky a mauled and immeasurable face. Eyes like balled-up leaves. Beyond the fields of scabby ice, the river swollen like an unlanced boil. Voice like a balled-up fist. In her hair, broken glass. Moon like a burned-down roach. Years a glove of hillside ice.

*

Sky an abandoned river. Eyes like unlanced boils. Beyond the glove of scabby fields, the hillside's burned and swollen face. Voice like a broken shiver. Hair a balled-up gray. Moon a year of broken glass. The mauled, immeasurable burning.

LIVES OF THE PHANTOM LIMB

ON THE OCCASION OF THE FIRST INTERSTELLAR LANDFILL

I don't know much about what separates the Control Group
from the other airborne contagions but a leak in the Fro-Zo-Sperm tank
will always mean a big mess to hose down. I know there is a great

alone-ness between the lacerated evening sky and where the boats,
toggled and docked, bob on the oil-slicked sea, but it is always
alone where I am, my Evaku-Suit damp and too tight and where I am

forever misplacing the numb chucks or leaving the Hydro-Float stuck
in the drawer, mixing up the salad forks with the other zip-locked
weapons. Tell me, is there really a hole in the sky and any point

to this yearning, is it a couch you have no use for,
abandoned to the rain, or obsolete like saline implants
and the art of the three-point turn. I don't know

how the lobster can have teeth in its stomach without
eating itself, which may be better than burning, and I don't
know how many times the world must eat itself, burn,

and start over—the ring slides back on the finger,
the elm reclothed in leaf, toxic spills retreating to the shores of our
hyperborean regret like the still-warm screen

of the mute T.V. or your imprint on the bed from a place
from where our love was already gone but still I could
almost touch you

BUNGEE JUMP

I don't need to know any more
about Time's omnivorous Be-In
to know that death is just a rose with all
the petals fallen off or that the mind
is useful in chess but makes pretty

lousy rain gear while the heart
never knows to hold or to fold but just lies
there, carp-like and twitching.
Better the animal dies of its wounds,

everything withered and gagged.
Better the antidote fails, the gums
hemorrhage when flossed,
the script washed-out with the tide and its

garbed machinations. All
is calamitous churning beneath
the lip of some unmanned prow.
Oh, the song he proposed to doesn't
sound so hot through the speakers at CVS;

in the light the chaps don't go so well
with the moon suit and madras tie.
I don't need to hear the story
of the body's maladroit hingings

or the radiometric entrails
of some deep sea fish to know that everything
between will eventually betray us as the clouds
betray the sun with their grandiose vexations as all
that year, our dumb selves lurched

calamitously away as spring's
befuddled nomenclature
lurching through the streets.
The figure led goat-like and braying
by the noose of its desire, desire

a thin voice heard through walls we will not
see again. I was ruined
when you got here; I'll be ruined
when you go. Better the sky dive's measured
by the height from which one falls.

LIVES OF VANISHING ISLANDS

Sometimes it's running in flippers
along the towpath, rooted
and gnarled, sometimes it's playing Beethoven's Ninth

on tambourine, the way the shoreline, if it must, will all
be subsumed by felonious tides, the way the body, if it must, will begin
to feed on itself, obsolete as we are all obsolete, doomed

as we are all doomed, so many numb chucks
in the repertoire of the clouds'
fraudulent gestures. I know we are not the only ones flanked

by abhorrent shadow as I know the universe is a glockenspiel
played continually out of tune, the way she had
to throw her wedding ring off the bridge

at Deception Pass because the body, if it must, will all be subsumed by
felonious tides the way the shoreline, if it must, will begin
to feed on itself, subsumed as we all must be subsumed, shadow

as we are all eventually shadow—one wakes in the half light
bestirred by inchoate whisperings; one sleeps past the baby's cry
that has torn the whole night through.

LIVES OF THE PROPHETS

First what we tried was deep-frying all the boats
but it got back to us the tape was jammed,
something off with the dubbing, and what
the edict said was *Keep buying all those oats.*
Next we tried spotting the reincarnated Magi
but couldn't pick them out from the rest
of the disgruntled urban youth.
It was all like that—dropping the house keys,
missing the sale on waffles, the endless ribbon of stars
rolling by on continuous play
as we struggled with the lack of funding
and the body's unreasonable demands.
Once we lay for hours in the anesthetizing cold,
beneath the mottled sky and its
unrepentant tonnage but just try getting a sign
from those hieroglyphic clouds,
obsessed as they are with morphing themselves
into bunny ears and coat-racks.
Spring comes on with its photogenic cruelty and all
we know for sure is steer clear
of The Outback's suspect crab. Lately I'm having
the dream again, of the face
and the giant swan, the sun imposed behind the trees
and burning itself alive.
Then the leaves and their sifted loosening,
the field threshed with wind--
Oh, I'm running through the palpitant wheat but not nearly
fast enough.

PERSEPHONE SPEAKS ON MOTHER'S DAY ABOUT HER FOURTEENTH SEASON OF CAPTIVITY IN THE UNDERWORLD

First I thought it was just getting past
the motion sensors and flares
but that was before Eternity's
tight-fisted decree, that is, prior
to the heyday of the single use mop.
From pretty much there on in it was
night sweats, bad skin, random bouts
of Seasonal Affective Disorder,
the kind of sanctioned groping
that goes on underground.
I was forced to abide by the tenets
of darkness, yes, although I could
go braless, my one consolation.
Mostly I got used to the thrummed
apertures of such longing, that kind of
okay-go-with-it feeling innate in our
stunned and apterous species, ourselves
but not fully ourselves, not unlike
the common wood frog, who freezes itself
in winter, its heart stopped,
yet unlike
the common wood frog, who thaws itself
in springtime, its heart set beating,
maybe rapturous, maybe mortal,
dormant yet not
quite dead, multiplying in the dark
like the globular agendas of fat cells
to emerge sweaty and gasping between
late summer's corn-fed thighs.
Come autumn's woody proboscis
and spring with its volatile hankerings,
the calendar just another LP
set on continuous play.
If you asked, my mom would say
the earth's green return to its
beating self would be her
second wish but the first
would be to touch me.

LIVES OF THE VANISHING TWIN

Not the wind's somnolent murmurs
As the finch resumes it hiatul warbling,
Not the tugged female aperture of what
Human failing, something exhumed
From the dig with the other carbon-dated matter
Or expunged, fractious and beating,
On the toggled rasure of waves,
Surely alone, possibly squalling
And clawed, pumped through with the bloated,
Corpuscular tide of what human bloodline in which
At least, chemically speaking, the brain's most similar
To the bowel and in which at least, chemically
Speaking, is always so close to death,
The way the wind's stunned fricatives heckle
The scantily-clad hydrangeas who dream of being
Carnivorous flowers, cantankerous and barbed,
O frayed exoskeleton of what
Human longing, the spent and vestigial creature
Still tethered to its side.

WINTER IN THE MAN-MADE ISLANDS

Dear Republican Victor, I am trying
to find a way to buy the recollection of snow,
the goose's throaty exodus

over the ravaged autumn fields,
sound of the leaves' wind-stunned departures
and the stratosphere heavy with dew,

slung with the displaced ions of wrecking balls
and the planet's atomic commands.
There are as many names for vanish

as there are forgeries of cloud,
the frog's adenoidal forays
in and out of the half-drained marsh.

Dear Vanquished arboreal shadow,
Dear feathers stuck with oil, I am trying
to buy a way to buy you back

LIVES OF VESTIGIAL ORGANS

View of the flaccid bathers,
View of Marty's clam shack and the ocean's
Hydraulic wreckage, its phosphorescent teeming
Hurled headfirst against the shore and what doesn't
Long to hurl itself headfirst
Against some shore; the flayed human heart
And its interminable pulsing,
The evening carrying on with it riotous
Masks of doom. Who knew
It would come to this, wandering a strip of beach
Beneath the badly-choreographed clouds,
En route to the fiefdom of sleep and its
Crenellated vault where each night the body stores
Its blunted instruments of need.
Once, a psychic told me I would live
And die by water.
What I've learned here mainly
Is that anything can be eaten:
The ruin of our breath.
This gyroscopic sky.
These nodules at my shoulders where
The flippers used to be.

LIVES OF THE PHANTOM LIMB

Sometimes it's missing the shape of his mouth
at three a.m., sometimes it's visions of falling
or Erica's dream of the giant breasts,
sometimes it's video poker
or taking thirteen showers a day,
observing his face in the clouds and their
flighty salutations, walking around,
buying Corn-Nuts and Drano
and skirts of wholly unsuitable length,
sometimes copious urgings and making a mess
of the canapés while all the while the heart
goes on with its terrible convulsions.
O ectoplasmic creature of inherently
flawed design, these tethers may look sturdy
but they will not last the night.

TALK RADIO

Dear Listener, I have been trying
to find a way to halt this pulsing
in my chest. And the rain-
I've yet to keep it
from its hydrophonic bleeps.
Perhaps, like me, you never intended
to make it this far,
the little holding us up
vaulted through the clouds'
volumetric displays.
Suppose I begin where the ground rose up
at the hinge of disbelief, those years
I divide before and aft the magnificent
freefall of childhood.
These days, I'm more likely waxing
or upgrading the bottom line
than saving cereal proofs-of-purchase
for a bathmat shaped like a duck.
Otherwise, not much
has changed: I've yet to master the art
of the three-point turn or the body's
de facto commands.
You'll still find me stretched-out in the tub
or lying prostrate on the couch
five days each month like clockwork
for the bulk of my reproductive years.
I wish, like earthworms,
we kept whole when split in two.
So little I know of this reddish flood
running from my vein.
Should I go incommunicado,
come find me in the fog.
Please. Please.
Do not leave me
here without you.

LIVES OF THE ALPHA MALE

First I hauled ass upstream
past the scores of hapless rubes
then it was Adios, Happy Trails, and I
was through the door. Tremendous
sense of pulsing. Security was nil.
Flash forward forty weeks to the hour
of my birth: Imagine Buick passed
through keyhole. Head secured in vise.
From there on in, it was touch and go
as I claimed the chronic scourge
of my birthright—Lotto stubs;
avarice; impure thoughts
of the waitress--dodging the sensitivity training
for the multi-district truck pull, struck
with pronged and thunderous yearnings
of the wholly physical kind. Thrust forward
then flung back in one big cosmic
game of Foosball, our kind swim upstream faster
but in the end we die off quick.
All I ask is that my soul mate come
equipped with movable limbs because our kind
swim upstream faster but in the end we die off quick.

OUIJA BOARD

Each day it thinks this must be the last time it can possibly haul itself
through the turnstile and into the dawn's
improvident shadow, mostly the body just lies
there, inert, in the mountainous In-Box
of its dreams, sometimes it will heave itself through the crenellated
night to run five miles beneath the city's invisible stars,
sometimes Hey, says the body, Let's go out and maim the faceless
multitudes but more often Hey, says the body, Let's just
lie here and space out on the goofy
similitudes of cloud, the body has never forgiven
the pair of gloved, avuncular hands that yanked it squalling
onto the table, it had wanted to breath underwater forever and Sure,
it had wanted to live forever but not really, Sure, it had wanted to love
forever but not really, now each time the body wakes
it thinks this must be the last time it can possibly
dream of the sofa made of tongues, the world a nest
of startled notes that sound like eat, and fuck, and maim, I love
you therefore I must maim you, says the body in situ, and fields of
carnivorous flowers will bloom inside its chest.

Handfasting in Spring

LIVING IN SIN

How like the moon's gouged-out face
the lover appears at night, how the nights,
like lovers, leave marks.
All through the shuttered hours the mice
have been up to their usual
nocturnal fisticuffs over the half-opened
bag of chips as sleep sputters in
and out through the half-opened, bloodless
gash of the mouth.

I think I will grow old by this water,
my face a web of hieroglyphs as seen
on the cracked walls of love's
bombed-out territories or the subterranean hinterlands
of the dead.

I know there are zones, the dog-eared,
paregoric recollections we will enter, pause,
and pass through , or leave to starve out
like the rabbit trapped by the foreleg
under a branch the storm had loosed-

in the woods,
by degrees,
felled, splayed, humming.

MYTHS ABOUT CERTAINTY

1. The ring slides back on the finger. 2. The house of the body is love. 3. The deposit on the hall is refundable. 4. Waterproof means *won't get wet*. 5. All doctors are alike. 6. The tap water is safe. 7. No news is good news. 8. The body is love's regret. 9. A cycle is twenty-eight days. 10. More about regret. 11. Flame-retardant means *won't catch fire*. 12. I will always love you, etc. 13. The ventilation system is adequate. 14. Shakespeare was a) Marlowe b) an asshole c) the artist formerly known as Prince. 15. Rug burn is a necessary evil. 16. The ring can be resized. 17. The flotation device will save us. 18. These lines are for office use only. 19. The treatment won't leave scars. 20. Courtesy is contagious. 21. The test results are valid. 22. Gone means *might come back*.

THE LATE MARRIAGE

Where once it had visions
of grandeur, neon drinks
downed late and once
only, it longs solely
to lie down between
the unmarred bodies
of its hosts.
It no longer insists
on spooking the horses
or painting a face
over its own.
Come long deathbeds,
smoke,
the dreams like bad meat,
spaces on earth
where nothing grows
and the many-fingered dark.
Put the dog out, let
the dog in. Years
like the screen door
wheezing on its hinge.

SONG OF THE STONE

The stone, the water, the body, the hand
The water, the woman, the body, the man
The body, the hold, the rising, the pulse
The hand, the surge, the woman, the crest
The grasp, the hold, the mouth, the surge
The hold, the pulse, the woman, the man
The mouth, the pulse, the rising, the crest
The surge, the woman, the rising, the child
The hand, the body, the water, the stone
The body, the woman, the rising, the child
The water, the mouth, the child, the surge
The stone, the water, the body, the hand

EARLY INDICATIONS OF THE THEORY OF EVERYTHING

Already the quorum of stars and their distant,
Apocryphal hum, already the field
Lashed with frost, the lightning's frenzied
Pyrotechnics, already the sound of water
And sea's voluminous displays, orbit
Of spinning and hurtling through the body's
Multitude failings. Soon organelle, soon ribosome,
Soon Golgi apparatus, soon body's rap sheet
Of forgeries and the vials on clinic shelves,
Soon eruption of fire ants like pus
From a ruptured boil, mosquito's suicidal
Forays, the zapper's sharp, unequivocal
Crack. Not the dream of lilies,
But of root-bulbs buried in snow.
Soon the faces of loved ones from where
Already the train has appeared.

LOVE POEM IN WHICH NOBODY SURVIVES

In August's stultified eye,
the a.c. sputters on and off.
Circuits blow. Dishes in the sink

grow spores. Deep inside her body's
tectonic reckonings, the corpus luteum
dissolves in the mute, unspoken
histories of the dead.

Each morning, the corrugated light
on the sheets, last night's dreams
absconded to their palatial hideaways
like displaced migrants on the lam.

She swears she'd seen his face
before--idling at the stoplight,
feeding quarters in the Coin-Op slot,

in the dimly-lit vestibules
of small-town chain motels.
He swears he never dreams, his sleep
plugged with night's lone ingrown hair.

Chapped lips, ash,
field you could hold a match to.

THIS THORN BUSH, MY THORN BUSH

All I have to say is that this lantern
    is the moon,

these hands, my hands,
    this the body, this the body gut-shot with need,

these eyes, your eyes,
    this tax bracket, our tax bracket,

this the wind, this the wind's
    tremulous whisper,

this the raw dirt, these the cherry trees
    glutted with bloom,

this blood, my blood,
    these our names, tectonic and thundering,

these wounds, our wounds,
    this the begetting, the Begotten still

unmoored at sea,
    these walls, our walls,

these thorns, our thorns,
    this the wild dog always at our backs,

but this dog, our dog

HANDFASTING IN SPRING

And the book said, In the beginning there was light and the light was good though it was but dim, a small spark in a big fire:

In the equinal light the world begins to stir and move in pairs, shed wool like casements from the winter's long and hapless body:

And from the beginning there was the Word, the Word which was Law, the word being light, dim flicker, small spark in a big fire and

through which we'd be forgiven everything—bad Pap smears, times you vamoosed without tipping, departures sans alibi, the myopic night vision of your small-town loves, the shoulda coulda woulda of the body's immeasurable failures like petty combustions held to light, small sparks in a big fire: The world is of one mind to bury its hatchet of remorse, to call to its friends on the shore, C'mon in, the water's fine, is of another to steal away and run off Godspeed to the mars where hordes of springtime peepers sound their propogant hullabaloos:

In May new things begin to root and move in the earth, earth the dupe, earth the long-suffering body, hapless light, small spark in a big fire, by turns soothed and held hostage by the specter of its fecundity, O springtime agendas of rupture, Go now, break forth or be broken:

And from the beginning there was the light and though it was good it was but dim, light the dupe, light the long and hapless body, its recollections scattered by springtime's muscular wind—her hair on the pillow, his foosteps' concussive reports—as surely the rivers go to ice and the ice to meet its reckoning, sure as the May sun hangs its bulbous apparition through the clouds, how it started: the light's undoing and the stuperous trudge unto, how it ends: small spark in a big fire

PROVIDENCE

I also remembered leaving
the station in the ancient blue
Chevy that pulled slightly to the right, direction
of the ocean always a low moan
in my ear even when asleep
in the loft bed I was afraid I'd fall
out of, the lamp retrieved from the dumpster
throwing off a dim light,
translucent, like skin held too long under-
water, the end of things getting
close but we couldn't see it and then I was
driving, your arm in a sling, the ocean
on my left now and the fog rolling in, Keep
going you told me and I said How far
just to see if it could sing?

PROCEDURES FOR THE SURGICAL FIELD

Don't write above this line: the silence there is golden

Don't bring what you can't carry: the evening has no hands

Don't cut in a clockwise manner: the body keeps no hours

Don't lean against the table: it has had to bear so much

Don't read up on the latest: some things are best unknown

Don't pump the flesh with saline: it is weak and full of holes

Don't bother to prep the surface: it is always at the ready

Don't hasten toward the door: the way is rigged and strewn with flowers

THE NAME OF THE BODY WHICH IS SLEEP

The name of the body which is sleep

the sleep of the body which is breath

the body of notes which is the breath

of the open window, *the sound*

of the body which is *I*, the door

of the sound which is *and*,

the breath of the note of the body

which is love, the sound *of the breath*

of the body which is *will*, the open

window, the note by the door *I will*

always love you and

SUPERSYMMETRY

Even now the waves' gallant receding
as still some whales go unharvested,

even now the restless continents
and the clamorous pingings in between,

just another amphibious planet crosshatched
with its giant, tsunamic reckonings

between the moon's silvery clavicle and the clouds,
feathered and whorled. So first it's the body's

clamorous hatchings and another
potentially-bicuspid zygote, the egg

shakes loose from its filament into a motorcade
of sperm and Voila, another clueless hominid

kicking the Coke machine in the hall.
Someday we will all be so many

vestigial organs under glass,
decomposing glial cells of our flogged

and sanctimonious forbears as the earth
carries on with its apoplectic music,

half Hallelujah chorus,
half Flight of the Bumblebee on kazoo.

Somewhere it is autumn,
the woods tossed and heady with pitch;

it is May, the sexy Black-Eyed Susans
knock-kneed in the wind.

Already somewhere it is too late, but wouldn't
you do it once all over,

wouldn't you spring the beast from its muzzle

EIGHT DAYS LATE

It's the dream again
of lead-footing it down the freeway
clear past the state line,
the sun a bombed-out husk
in the gathering light
of a three-quarter moon.
It's the waking again to the world
which is a hard and wild place
and to coffee slicked with grease,
love a clutch of gnarled misgivings.
Outside, the scabby trees
and their defoliated bodies brace against
November's spate of wind, a dry
warmed-over breath;
In the body's venomous hatchings
you're a poppy quickened in frost
but go on speaking
of other things, like the weather
and will it hold.

YOU AND ME AT THE HINTERLANDS CORRAL

First imagine water, the scene where all
this is happening, we were lounging on the pagoda
where waiters were serving drinks, no,
we're at the Tri-county fairgrounds ogling your first-place steer
and reddish mud is gathering on your wingtips or slingback heels,
no, it's only your skin that's white and red is what's
coming out because we're slumped forward in the totaled Saab
that's somehow wrapped around the elm, wait,
it's the chicken evisceration plant and we're ankle-deep
in blood because a third-generation gizzard-splitter
has suddenly opened fire, someone is yelling, Christ, Linda, not
this again or Tom, don't leave me, I can't
live without you, etc., we borrowed time, stole time,
no, we bought it on the installment plan, you were the end, no,
the means, no, the gutted deer swaddled to the hood,
there was a hailstorm full-force when we finally
reached the highway, no, it was scattered heavy shelling
outside the bunker all night, you were at the other
shore where none of this was happening, no, you
were the wind-torn island I had to die
to reach.

Robyn Art is a native of Lincoln, Massachusetts. Recent poems have appeared in *Slope, The Hat, Conduit, Slipstream, Gulf Coast, The New Delta Review, Wicked Alice, The Burnside Review,* and *canwehaveourballback.com*, as well as in the forthcoming anthology, *The Bedside Guide To No Tell Motel: Second Floor* (No Tell Books, Reb Livingston and Molly Arden, editors, 2008). Nominated five times for the Pushcart Prize, she  received Finalist honors in 2003, and has received grants from the *Vermont Studio Center*, *The Academy of American Poets,* and the *Jentel Arts Foundation* and has also been selected as a Finalist for the 2004 Kore Press First Book Award and the 2005 Sawtooth Poetry Prize. A text-visual collaboration with artist Robin Barcus, entitled, *Dear American Love Child, Yours, The Beautiful Undead* will be published by Dancing Girl Press in Winter 2008. She is the author of the chapbooks *Degrees of Being There* (Boneworld Press, May 2003,) *Vestigial Portions of the Dead Sea Scrolls* (Dancing Girl Press, September 2006) the text/visual collaboration *Scenes From The Body* (Dancing Girl Press, April 2007) as well as the online chapbooks *The Last Time I Saw Bonnie Blue* and *Body The Non-Body* (ensemblejcurine.com). She lives in Brooklyn with her young daughter, Titania.

DUSIE PRESS BOOKS

CORNSTARCH FIGURINE, ELIZABETH TREADWELL $13.00

THE SINGERS, LOGAN RYAN SMITH, $13.00

THE STUNT DOUBLE IN WINTER, ROBYN ART $13.00

forthcoming

THE BUTTERFLIES AND THE BURNINGS, ANNE BLONSTEIN

IN THE BIRD MUSEUM, Kristy Bowen

laws Jen Hofer

F-E-S-C-U-E, Paul Klinger

:ab ovo: Jenn McCreary

Strata, Joe Ross

www.ingramcontent.com/pod-product-compliance
Lightning Source LLC
LaVergne TN
LVHW011210080426
835508LV00007B/715